LOW
GI
COOK
BOOK

LOW GI COOK BOOK

**Over 70 delicious recipes to help
you lose weight and gain health**

Louise Blair

hamlyn

An Hachette Livre UK Company

First published in Great Britain in 2008 by
Hamlyn, a division of Octopus Publishing Group Ltd
2–4 Heron Quays, London E14 4JP

ISBN 978-0-600-61768-6

A CIP catalogue record for this book is available from the British Library.

Printed and bound in Great Britain by Mackays of Chatham

10 9 8 7 6 5 4 3 2 1

Notes
Standard level spoon measures are used in all recipes
1 tablespoon = one 15 ml spoon
1 teaspoon = one 5 ml spoon

Both metric and imperial measurements are given for the recipes. Use one set of measurements only, not a mixture of both.

Ovens should be preheated to the specified temperature. If using a fan-assisted oven, follow the manufacturer's instructions for adjusting the time and temperature. Grills should also be preheated.

This book includes dishes made with nuts and nut derivatives. It is advisable for those with known allergic reactions to nuts and nut derivatives and those who may be potentially vulnerable to these allergies, such as pregnant and nursing mothers, invalids, the elderly, babies and children, to avoid dishes made with nuts and nut oils. It is also prudent to check the labels of preprepared ingredients for the possible inclusion of nut derivatives.

The Department of Health advises that eggs should not be consumed raw. This book contains some dishes made with raw or lightly cooked eggs. It is prudent for more vulnerable people such as pregnant and nursing mothers, invalids, the elderly, babies and young children to avoid uncooked or lightly cooked dishes made with eggs.

Meat and poultry should be cooked thoroughly. To test if poultry is cooked, pierce the flesh through the thickest part with a skewer or fork – the juices should run clear, never pink or red.

All the recipes in this book have been analysed by a professional nutritionist. The analysis refers to each serving.

Contents

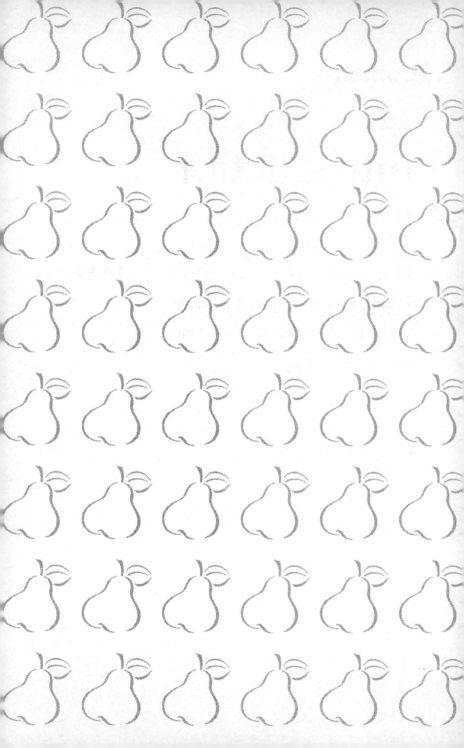

Introduction

Over the following pages you will learn about the benefits of switching to a low-GI diet. By sticking to a few simple rules you can enjoy the many health rewards it can bring without having to compromise on the taste or variety of your meals.

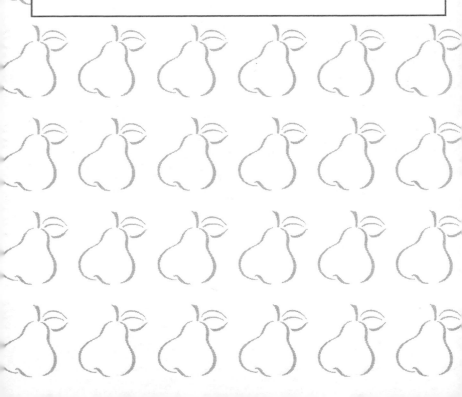

What is **GI**?

Put very simply, the glycaemic index measures how the food you eat reacts in your body. When you follow a low-GI diet, you choose foods that create only a positive reaction.

The majority of the foods we eat come from one main food group – carbohydrates, more specifically from white bread, potatoes, cakes, biscuits and sugary treats. While they taste good and are easy to eat, these foods create reactions in our bodies that put the entire system out of balance. The result of this imbalance is day-to-day problems, such as fatigue, mood swings and sugar cravings, plus an increased risk of a number of different health problems in the future. By basing your diet around the glycaemic index, you will stop all the confusion and allow your body to develop a sense of balance.

Fuelling your body
Your body requires a lot of energy to deal with all the stresses and strains of modern life, and its preferred fuel is a sugar called glucose, which it makes from the starches and sugars (carbohydrates) found in food. Glucose is made in the liver after the food has been digested in the stomach. The converted glucose is then sent to the body's cells where it is either burned immediately as we run, walk or even think, or stored in the muscles and fat stores for later use. This happens with almost every food that contains carbohydrates, whether it is a plate of spinach or a plate of doughnuts. However, different foods affect the speed with which this reaction happens, and, in very basic terms, the glycaemic index is a measure of that speed. Foods with a high glycaemic index (known as high-GI foods) are converted rapidly to glucose in the body, while foods with a low glycaemic index (low-GI foods) are converted more slowly.

The missing link
A hormone called insulin provides the missing link in this process. When glucose is released into the bloodstream, insulin takes it to

where it's needed. If the glucose is released slowly, moderate levels of insulin are released and have time to 'think' about where that glucose is needed most and send it there. However, if high levels of glucose enter the bloodstream, the body panics – too much glucose can be harmful. To compensate, the body releases high levels of insulin, which quickly transfer the glucose to the fat stores where it can do no harm. If this happens too often, it can lead to weight gain as well as the cells that normally respond to glucose becoming resistant to its signals. This means that less glucose is taken to where it's needed, and it remains in the bloodstream, causing cell damage, which contributes to ageing and furring of the arteries.

About turn
By switching to a low-GI diet and ensuring you eat only foods that cause a gentle rise in glucose in your bloodstream, you can reverse this process and prevent a panic reaction in your system. The results can positively affect the condition and function of every part of your body, from your heart to your skin, and will boost weight loss.

All foods are not equal
When you are choosing a GI eating plan, it is important that you know which foods are best to choose. There are six main factors that determine the GI of a food.

❶ Does it contain carbohydrate?
Pure protein foods, such as meat, fish, poultry and eggs, and pure fats, such as oils, butter and margarine, contain no carbohydrate, so the effect they have on glucose production is negligible. These foods are therefore low GI.

❷ How much starch does it contain and in what form?
Starch is the easiest ingredient for our body to turn into glucose. In raw foods, where this starch is generally in compact particles, the body finds it difficult to break down. However, if these particles are disturbed (for example, milling to make flour), the body finds it easier to digest them and therefore turns them into glucose faster.

❸ How much fibre does it contain?
Fibre makes the body break food down more slowly, which is one of

the reasons why beans and pulses (which are wrapped in a fibrous shell) have such a low GI.

❹ What kind of sugar does it contain?

There are four main types of sugar. Foods high in glucose (such as sports drinks) need no conversion, so they raise blood sugar rapidly, while fructose (the sugar in fruit) and lactose (the main sugar in dairy products) convert slowly. This gives the majority of the foods that contain fructose or lactose a low GI. The fourth sugar, sucrose, has a medium GI.

❺ Does it contain fat?

Fat has no effect on glucose itself, but it does slow the speed of food from the stomach to the liver, in turn slowing glucose production.

❻ How acidic is it?

Citrus fruits are an example of foods that contain acid ingredients, in this case citric acid. Other acidic ingredients include lactic acid in milk products. Acidity slows a food's progress through the system and therefore the rate at which it converts into glucose.

GI facts about carbohydrates

If you follow a GI diet the biggest changes you will probably make to your regular diet are to the following six foods: bread, breakfast cereal, grains, pasta, potatoes and rice. It is often these foods that make up the majority of our diet, and they are also the easiest to convert into glucose. Don't panic though. The low-GI diet doesn't completely ban starchy carbohydrates. The idea is to switch your choices to those that have the lowest impact on your blood sugar levels.

Bread

Many of us tend to eat a lot of bread. This is fine as long you opt for low-GI breads that are high in fibre – Granary or wholegrain are best, as the hard husk around the grains slows glucose conversion. Breads made from an ingredient with a lower GI than wheat are also a good choice. These include soya bread and rye bread.

Breakfast cereals

It's important to eat breakfast as it prevents you getting hunger pangs that lead you to eating less-nutritious snacks mid-morning. However, a high-GI breakfast cereal is just as likely to leave you hungry as having no breakfast at all. You should avoid cereals that have been processed or have high levels of added sugar or honey, and instead go for high-fibre cereals, such as bran or traditional porridge oats.

Grains

Grains are subject to minimal processing, so most have a low GI. They are also generally high in essential B vitamins and vital minerals, such as magnesium or phosphorus. Barley, buckwheat, bulgar wheat, millet and quinoa (the gluten-free seeds of an annual plant) are all low GI, while couscous is medium GI. They can all be used instead of potatoes or rice as a side dish and are also very easy and quick to prepare.

Pasta

Surprisingly, almost all pastas are low-GI foods. This is because the flour used to make them (durum wheat) contains protein, which slows its digestion. The starch particles in pasta are left fairly intact, which also slows things down. The problem with pasta is that we generally eat much larger portions than recommended, thereby increasing the amount of glucose produced. It's best to eat pasta *al dente* – the softer the pasta, the higher its GI rating. The exception is gluten-free pasta. This is made with wheat-free flour, so doesn't have the protein protection provided by durum wheat.

Noodles

Some noodles are made from a more glutinous form of wheat flour, so are best avoided. However, glass noodles, cellophane noodles and many types of harusame noodle are made of mung bean starch and have a very low GI rating.

Potatoes

Potatoes may be a great source of vitamin C, potassium and the anti-ageing nutrient glutathione, but they score badly on the GI plan. This is believed to be due to their high starch content, which increases if new potatoes are left on the plant to grow. In fact, new potatoes are the only potatoes to have a low GI, so choose these whenever possible, or substitute potatoes with another, low-GI, carbohydrate. The other option is to use sweet potatoes, which have a medium GI and can be prepared in much the same way as regular potatoes.

Rice

The GI content of rice is dependent upon which type of starch it contains – amylose, which is tightly bonded together, or amylopectin, which is more branched out. Rices high in amylose have a lower GI.

Carbohydrate snacks

Most snacks have a high GI, and even savoury snacks can raise glucose levels too quickly. However, snacking is actually encouraged when you are on a low-GI diet, because eating a small meal or snack every two hours keeps blood sugar levels even more stable than eating three large meals a day. Try snacking on nuts, seeds, fruit, yogurt – or a little chocolate. Yes, you may be surprised to learn that chocolate has a low GI, due to a high concentration of dairy products, a high fat content and also its sucrose content, which converts into glucose at a slow rate.

GI facts about **fruit** and **vegetables**

Fruit

As a general rule, fruit is a low-GI food. The main sugar in many fruit is fructose, and this has to be converted into glucose before it can be used by the body, thus preventing the sudden peak in blood sugar that can cause the rapid release of insulin.

What affects the GI of a fruit?

Acidity Generally, the more acidic a particular fruit is, the lower its GI.

Fibre content Fruit with the highest soluble fibre content (such as apples and pears) are those with the lowest GI.

Fructose content Most fruit contains a mixture of three sugars: fructose, sucrose and glucose. The more fructose (and less glucose) a fruit contains, the lower its GI.

Processing Canning softens the fibrous strands in fruit, making it easier to break down and slightly increasing the rate at which glucose is created. Fruit is also often canned in syrup, which can contain fast-release sugars and raise GI from low to medium. Fruit juice also has a higher GI because the fibre has been removed.

Vegetables

Like fruit, the majority of vegetables are low-GI foods. Despite the fact that many are classed as carbohydrate foods, the actual amount of carbohydrates they contain is very small. In addition to this, most vegetables are very high in fibre, which is a GI inhibitor. There are some exceptions to this general rule, such as starchy root vegetables (beetroot, parsnips and swedes), and sweet vegetables (pumpkins and squashes), which are medium- or high-GI foods. This doesn't mean you should never eat these vegetables, but you must remember to keep the portions moderate and not eat them at every meal. If you bear this in mind there is no reason why you should ban vegetables with a high-GI entirely from your diet.

GI facts about **protein** foods

As we have seen, pure protein foods contain no carbohydrate and therefore have a low GI. However, foods that contain high levels of protein but also some level of carbohydrate, have a higher GI rating.

Beans and pulses

A diet containing regular servings of legumes has been shown to lead to lower cholesterol levels and also to help balance hormones in women, thereby possibly reducing the risk of breast cancer – so we should all be eating more of them. Most beans and pulses (or legumes) have a low GI because of the fibrous coating around them, which slows conversion.

Dairy products

Many dairy products contain the sugar lactose, which is converted into glucose in the body. However, like fructose, lactose is converted slowly, meaning that dairy products, such as milk, cheese and yogurt, are low-GI foods.

Nuts and seeds

The combination of protein and fats gives nuts and seeds their low GI. Some nutritionists have described seeds as a superfood, and they can easily be eaten by the handful as a snack or sprinkled over salads. Remember, too, that spreads and dips made from nuts and seeds, such as peanut butter and tahini, will also have a low GI.

When **low**-GI meets **high**

No one wants to eat the same foods every day, and the great thing about the GI eating plan is that no food is completely banned. There are, however, a few simple rules to follow when you eat a high-GI food.

The rules

1 When you eat a high-GI food, watch your portion size. The more you eat, the greater the amount of glucose that will be produced.

2 Every time you eat a high-GI food you should accompany it with at least two low-GI foods of the same or a larger quantity to lower the average GI. Ideally, one of the accompanying foods should be a protein food and the other should be fruit or vegetables. So, for example, if you have 25 g (1 oz) of high-GI cornflakes for breakfast, you should accompany this with 100 ml (3½ oz) of skimmed milk and a sliced peach.

3 Avoid eating more than one high-GI food or two medium-GI foods in any one day – and, if at all possible, eat fewer than this. By sticking to this simple approach you will be giving your body the chance to really get back into balance.

4 Try to add something acidic to your meal whenever possible. In the same way that acid integrated into a food slows its conversion to glucose, so does acid added to a high-GI food. So, for example, you could accompany a main meal containing rice with a fresh side salad topped with a vinaigrette dressing.

10 reasons to eat low-GI foods

1 Your heart will thank you. According to research conducted at Harvard University, women with a high intake of refined carbohydrates have 10 per cent less good cholesterol in their bloodstream. Good cholesterol helps keep the heart healthy.

2 High levels of homocysteine are linked to heart problems and the development of Alzheimer's disease in later life. By taking simple measures, such as swapping rice for wholegrains, your levels of homocysteine can fall dramatically.

3 A diet rich in high-GI foods may increase the risk of breast cancer. The reason is that high insulin levels trigger an increase in insulin-like growth hormones, which can encourage breast cancer cells.

4 Health experts recommend eating 25–30 g (about 1 oz) of fibre a day. A high-fibre content is a contributing factor in making a food low GI. Increased fibre consumption will boost weight loss, because fibre helps sweep fat calories out of the system.

5 Many determatologists believe that refined carbohydrates trigger inflammation of the skin, which can affect the collagen and elastin fibres that keep skin firm.

6 Reducing insulin levels can help acne and oily skin. High insulin levels lead to the release of higher levels of androgens in the system, which trigger excess sebum production.

7 According to the World Health Organization, the number of people suffering from diabetes will double by the year 2030. Switching to low-GI diets could cut the number of potential sufferers dramatically.

8 A low-GI diet can reduce the risk of stroke. Women who switched just one serving of refined carbohydrates to wholegrains each day cut their risk of stroke by 40 per cent, say researchers at Harvard University.

9 When fighting illness, the average white blood cell can destroy about 14 germs in an hour. However, when exposed to 100 g (3½ oz) of sugar, that number falls to 1.4 germs per hour and stays that way for two hours. Low-GI eating will potentially cut the risks of ailments such as colds and flu.

10 Many exercisers think they need high-sugar bursts to fuel their bodies, but sticking to a low-GI diet actually increases endurance.

Low-GI portions for high-GI foods

Potatoes 100 g (3½ oz)
Rice 75 g (3 oz) cooked weight, roughly 25 g (1 oz) dried
Bread 1–2 slices
Breakfast cereals 25 g (1 oz)
Root vegetables 100 g (3½ oz)
Popcorn and pretzels 25 g (1 oz)

Start the day

From a quick bite to a hearty meal, a good
breakfast really does set you up for the day ahead.
There's plenty here to suit every appetite and
time constraint.

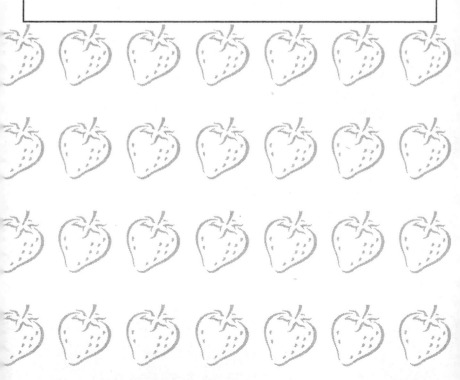

Wild mushroom omelette

25 g (1 oz) butter
200 g (7 oz) wild mushrooms, trimmed and sliced
8 large eggs, beaten
2 tablespoons chopped parsley
50 g (2 oz) Gruyère cheese, grated
pepper
Granary toast, to serve

preparation: 10 minutes
cooking: about 20 minutes
serves: 4

nutritional values per serving
Kcals: 282 (1172 kj)
Protein: 19 g
Carb: 0 g
Fat: 23 g

1 Melt a little of the butter in an omelette pan, add the mushrooms and sauté for 5-6 minutes until cooked and any moisture has evaporated. Remove the mushrooms from the pan and set them aside.

2 Melt a little more butter in the same pan and add one-quarter of the beaten egg. Season well with pepper and stir with a wooden spoon, bringing the cooked egg to the centre of the pan and allowing the runny egg to flow to the edge and cook.

3 When there is only a little liquid egg left, sprinkle over a quarter of the mushrooms, parsley and Gruyère, fold the omelette over and tip on to a warm serving plate. Repeat with the remaining ingredients. Serve with Granary toast.

Easy corned beef hash

1 teaspoon olive oil
1 onion, chopped
350 g (11½ oz) cooked new potatoes, roughly chopped
350 g (11½ oz) corned beef, roughly chopped
1 tablespoon chopped parsley
Worcestershire sauce, to taste
pepper
thick Granary toast, to serve

preparation: 10 minutes
cooking: 10 minutes
serves: 4

nutritional values per serving
Kcals: 277 (1162 kj)
Protein: 25 g
Carb: 19 g
Fat: 12 g

1 Heat the oil in a large, nonstick frying pan. Add the onion and fry for 2–3 minutes until softened.

2 Add the potatoes and corned beef and continue to fry for 6–7 minutes, turning the mixture occasionally so that parts of it become crisp.

3 Stir the parsley through the hash, then season to taste with Worcestershire sauce and pepper. Serve with thick Granary toast. For a change, you could also serve the hash topped with a poached egg.

Creamy herby scrambled eggs on rye

8 large eggs
4 tablespoons milk
15 g (½ oz) polyunsaturated margarine
2 tablespoons light cream cheese
2 tablespoons chopped mixed tender herbs (such as parsley,
    oregano and chives)
salt (optional) and pepper
4 thick slices of rye bread, to serve

preparation: 5 minutes
cooking: 5 minutes
serves: 4

nutritional values per serving
Kcals: 300 (1252 kj)
Protein: 19 g
Carb: 15 g
Fat: 19 g

1 In a bowl beat together the eggs and milk and season with salt, if liked, and pepper. Heat the margarine in a nonstick frying pan, add the egg mixture and stir constantly with a wooden spoon for a few minutes until the eggs are softly set.

2 Remove the pan from the heat and stir in the cream cheese and herbs, then serve on thick slices of rye bread.

Pear pancakes

50 g (2 oz) polyunsaturated margarine, melted
50 g (2 oz) self-raising flour
50 g (2 oz) wholemeal self-raising flour
25 g (1 oz) oatmeal
1 tablespoon caster sugar
2 eggs, lightly beaten
275 ml (9 fl oz) buttermilk
milk, for thinning (optional)
oil, for brushing
6 pears, peeled, cored and chopped
pinch of cinnamon
1 tablespoon water

preparation: 10 minutes
cooking: about 20 minutes
serves: 4 (makes 12 small pancakes)

nutritional values per serving
Kcals: 378 (1585 kj)
Protein: 10 g
Carb: 52 g
Fat: 16 g

1 In a bowl beat together the margarine, flours, oatmeal, sugar, eggs and buttermilk until smooth, adding a little milk if the mixture looks very thick.

2 Brush a nonstick frying pan with a little oil and heat. Add a ladleful of batter to the pan and cook for 2 minutes on each side until golden. Remove the pancake from the pan and keep warm. Repeat with the remaining batter mixture.

3 Meanwhile, place the pears and cinnamon in a small saucepan with the water. Cover and cook gently for 2–3 minutes until just tender. Serve the pancakes with the cooked pears.

tip
If you can't find buttermilk, mix together equal quantities of natural yogurt and skimmed milk.

Buckwheat pancakes with banana and cream cheese

50 g (2 oz) plain flour
50 g (2 oz) buckwheat flour
300 ml (½ pint) skimmed milk
1 egg, beaten
oil, for frying
100 g (3½ oz) light cream cheese
4 small bananas, sliced

preparation: 10 minutes
cooking: 10 minutes
serves: 4 (makes 4 large or 8 small pancakes)

nutritional values per serving
Kcals: 276 (1160 kj)
Protein: 10 g
Carb: 43 g
Fat: 8 g

1 Sift the flours together into a bowl, tipping any bran in the sieve back into the bowl. Whisk together the milk and egg and gradually add them to the flour, beating to form a smooth batter.

2 Brush a nonstick frying pan with a little oil and heat. Add a ladleful of batter to the pan and cook for 1–2 minutes on each side until golden. Remove the pancake from the pan and keep warm. Repeat with the remaining batter mixture.

3 Smooth a little cream cheese over each pancake and top with some sliced banana. Fold in half and serve.

Porridge with apricot purée

175 g (6 oz) rolled oats
750 ml (1¼ pints) skimmed milk or water
2 teaspoons soft brown sugar
200 g (7 oz) ready-to-eat dried apricots
300 ml (½ pint) orange juice

preparation: 10 minutes
cooking: 10 minutes
serves: 4

nutritional values per serving
Kcals: 344 (1460 kj)
Protein: 14 g
Carb: 66 g
Fat: 5 g

tip
As an alternative you could
serve the porridge with
poached fruit of your choice,
such as cherries or plums.

1 Place the oats, milk or water and sugar in a saucepan and bring to the boil. Reduce the heat and simmer for about 10 minutes until the oats are softened and the required consistency is reached.

2 Meanwhile, place the apricots and orange juice in a separate saucepan and bring to the boil. Reduce the heat and simmer for 10 minutes. Transfer to a food processor or blender and process until smooth. Serve the purée over the porridge.

Blueberry, peach and citrus salad with wholegrain yogurt

200 g (7 oz) blueberries
2 oranges, segmented
2 grapefruits, segmented
2 peaches, halved, stoned and sliced
50 g (2 oz) toasted wholegrains
300 ml (½ pint) natural yogurt
2 teaspoons maple syrup

preparation: 10 minutes
serves: 4

nutritional values per serving
Kcals: 183 (775 kj)
Protein: 7 g
Carb: 38 g
Fat: 1 g

Divide the prepared fruit among 4 bowls. Mix together the remaining ingredients and spoon over the fruit. Serve.

nutritional tip
Oranges are a good source of folates. These are essential to a baby's development in the womb and for the formation of red blood cells in adults. All citrus fruits are high in vitamin C as well, which helps fight infection.

tip
If you can't find wholegrains in your local health-food shop or supermarket, you can replace them with the same weight of toasted mixed nuts.

Toasted fruity muesli

100 g (3½ oz) jumbo oats, toasted
25 g (1 oz) wheatgerm
25 g (1 oz) toasted mixed seeds (such as pumpkin, sunflower and
    sesame)
15 g (½ oz) hazelnuts, toasted and roughly chopped
50 g (2 oz) ready-to-eat dried apricots
50 g (2 oz) dried cranberries
3 dried figs, chopped
semi-skimmed milk, to serve

preparation: 10 minutes
serves: 4

nutritional values per serving
Kcals: 293 (1237 kj)
Protein: 9 g
Carb: 48 g
Fat: 9 g

Combine all the ingredients in a large mixing bowl. Serve in cereal bowls with semi-skimmed milk.

tip
This muesli is also delicious served with natural yogurt and chopped fresh fruit, such as pears and apples, or summer berries.

Basic smoothie mixture

1 small banana
150 ml (¼ pint) low-fat natural yogurt
200 ml (7 fl oz) skimmed milk
few drops of vanilla extract

preparation: 5 minutes
serves: 1

nutritional values per serving
Kcals: 226 (956 kj)
Protein: 15 g
Carb: 40 g
Fat: 2 g

Whiz together all the ingredients in a food processor or blender until smooth. Serve in a tall glass.

Tropical fruit smoothie

½ ripe mango
Basic Smoothie Mixture (see opposite)
1 passion fruit

preparation: 5 minutes
serves: 1

nutritional values per serving
Kcals: 276 (1160 kj)
Protein: 16 g
Carb: 51 g
Fat: 2 g

Add the flesh of ½ ripe mango to the basic mixture. Whiz together all the ingredients in a food processor or blender until smooth, then stir through the flesh of 1 passion fruit. Serve in a tall glass.

Summer berry smoothie

75 g (3 oz) mixed summer berries
Basic Smoothie Mixture (see page 34)

preparation: 5 minutes
serves: 1

nutritional values per serving
Kcals: 247 (1036 kj)
Protein: 16 g
Carb: 43 g
Fat: 2 g

Add the mixed summer berries (thawed if frozen) to the basic mixture. Whiz together all the ingredients in a food processor or blender until smooth. Serve in a tall glass.

Apple and oat smoothie

1 apple, cored and chopped
2 teaspoons clear honey
2 tablespoons muesli
Basic Smoothie Mixture (see page 34)

preparation: 5 minutes
serves: 1

nutritional values per serving
Kcals: 415 (1750 kj)
Protein: 19 g
Carb: 80 g
Fat: 4 g

Add the apple, honey and muesli to the basic mixture. Whiz together all the ingredients in a food processor or blender until smooth. Serve in a tall glass.

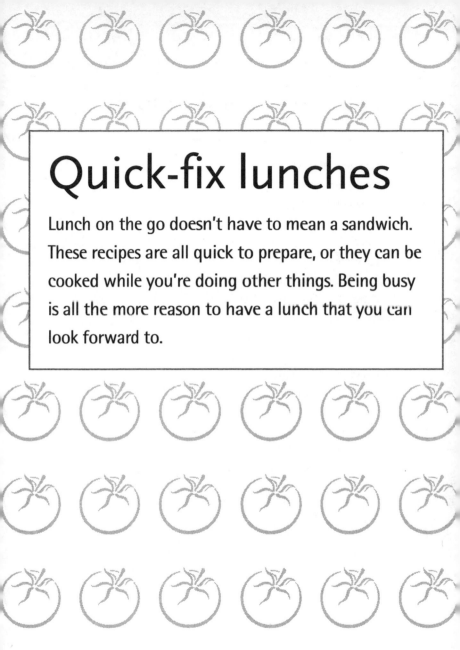

Quick-fix lunches

Lunch on the go doesn't have to mean a sandwich. These recipes are all quick to prepare, or they can be cooked while you're doing other things. Being busy is all the more reason to have a lunch that you can look forward to.

Summer vegetable soup

1 teaspoon olive oil
1 leek, finely sliced
1 large potato, chopped
450 g (14½ oz) mixed summer vegetables (such as peas, asparagus,
    broad beans and courgettes)
2 tablespoons chopped mint
900 ml (1½ pints) vegetable stock
2 tablespoons light crème fraîche
salt (optional) and pepper

preparation: 10 minutes
cooking: 15 minutes
serves: 4

nutritional values per serving
Kcals: 136 (566 kj)
Protein: 6 g
Carb: 17 g
Fat: 5 g

1 Heat the oil in a medium-sized saucepan, add the leek and fry for 3–4 minutes until softened.

2 Add the vegetables to the pan with the mint and the stock and bring to the boil. Reduce the heat and simmer for 10 minutes.

3 Transfer the soup to a food processor or blender and process until smooth. Tip back into the pan with the crème fraîche and season with salt, if liked, and pepper. Heat through gently and serve.

Corn chowder

1 teaspoon olive oil
1 onion, chopped
450 g (14½ oz) potatoes, chopped
600 ml (1 pint) vegetable stock
300 ml (½ pint) milk
1 bay leaf
325 g (11 oz) can sweetcorn kernels, drained
2 large tomatoes, chopped
2 tablespoons chopped parsley
salt (optional) and pepper

preparation: 15 minutes
cooking: 25 minutes
serves: 4

nutritional values per serving
Kcals: 265 (1123 kj)
Protein: 8 g
Carb: 50 g
Fat: 5 g

1 Heat the oil in a medium-sized saucepan, add the onion and fry for 2–3 minutes until beginning to soften. Add the potatoes and continue to fry for 2 minutes, then add the stock, milk and bay leaf. Bring to the boil, reduce the heat and simmer gently for 15 minutes.

2 Add the sweetcorn and tomatoes and continue to simmer for 5 minutes, then remove the bay leaf. Transfer the soup to a food processor or blender and process until smooth. Return to the pan with the parsley and season with salt, if liked, and pepper. Heat through gently and serve.

Chicken and pearl barley broth

1 teaspoon oil
2 leeks, finely sliced
1 carrot, chopped
1 celery stick, chopped
250 g (8 oz) lean boneless, skinless chicken, finely sliced
25 g (1 oz) pearl barley, prepared and cooked according to pack
    instructions
900 ml (1½ pints) chicken stock
2 tablespoons chopped parsley
salt (optional) and pepper

preparation: 15 minutes
cooking: 35 minutes
serves: 4

nutritional values per serving
Kcals: 122 (513 kj)
Protein: 15 g
Carb: 8 g
Fat: 3 g

1 Heat the oil in a medium-sized saucepan, add the leeks, carrot and celery and fry for 3–4 minutes until beginning to soften. Add the chicken and continue to fry for 2 minutes. Add the barley and stock and bring to the boil. Reduce the heat and simmer for 20 minutes.

2 Transfer half the soup to a food processor or blender and process until smooth. Return to the pan with the parsley and season well with salt, if liked, and pepper. Heat through and serve.

Cauliflower and cumin soup

1 teaspoon oil
1 onion, chopped
1 garlic clove, crushed
1 teaspoon cumin seeds
1 cauliflower, cut into florets
1 large potato, chopped
450 ml (¾ pint) vegetable stock
450 ml (¾ pint) milk
2 tablespoons light crème fraîche
2 tablespoons chopped fresh coriander
salt (optional) and pepper

preparation: 10 minutes
cooking: 20 minutes
serves: 4

nutritional values per serving
Kcals: 152 (640 kj)
Protein: 8 g
Carb: 19 g
Fat: 6 g

1 Heat the oil in a medium-sized saucepan, add the onion, garlic and cumin seeds and fry for 3–4 minutes. Add the cauliflower, potato, stock and milk and bring to the boil. Reduce the heat and simmer for 15 minutes.

2 Transfer the soup to a food processor or blender and process until smooth. Stir through the crème fraîche and coriander and season with salt, if liked, and pepper. Heat through and serve.

nutritional tip
Used extensively in Middle Eastern and Indian cooking, cumin seeds were traditionally believed to be good for the digestive system, and science has since backed up this claim. To release their distinctive aroma and flavour, cumin seeds should always be roasted or fried.

tip
This soup is delicious served with multigrain bread, topped with melted Gruyère cheese.

Gazpacho

1 thick slice of day-old white bread
2 tablespoons white wine vinegar
450 g (14½ oz) ripe tomatoes, skinned and chopped
1 garlic clove, crushed
300 ml (½ pint) passata
300 ml (½ pint) water
few drops of Tabasco sauce
1 small red pepper, cored, deseeded and chopped
½ cucumber, chopped
½ red onion, finely chopped
handful of basil, torn
1 tablespoon extra virgin olive oil
salt (optional) and pepper

preparation: 15 minutes, plus chilling
serves: 4

nutritional values per serving
Kcals: 123 (520 kj)
Protein: 5 g
Carb: 20 g
Fat: 4 g

1 Tear the bread into pieces and soak it in the vinegar. Place the tomatoes, garlic, passata, soaked bread and water in a food processor or blender and process until smooth. Season with salt, if liked, and pepper, and add Tabasco sauce to taste.

2 Cover and chill in the refrigerator for at least 1 hour. Serve the soup topped with a mixture of the red pepper, cucumber, onion and basil, then drizzle over a little oil.

Aubergine and chickpea pâté

1 tablespoon olive oil
1 aubergine, chopped
200 g (7 oz) can chickpeas, rinsed and drained
100 g (3½ oz) light cream cheese
3 spring onions, finely sliced
2 tablespoons chopped mixed herbs (such as parsley, basil and
    chives)
salt (optional) and pepper
to serve
crudités
toasted wholemeal pitta bread

preparation: 10 minutes
cooking: 10 minutes
serves: 4

nutritional values per serving
Kcals: 140 (588 kj)
Protein: 7 g
Carb: 11 g
Fat: 8 g

1 Heat the oil in a nonstick saucepan, add the aubergine and fry for 7–8 minutes until tender. Don't add any more oil as this is plenty. Leave to cool.

2 Transfer the aubergine to a food processor or blender with all the remaining ingredients and process until almost smooth but retaining a little texture. Serve the pâté with crudités and toasted pitta bread.

Griddled haloumi on bulgar wheat and beetroot salad

4 tablespoons chopped mixed herbs
grated rind and juice of 1 lemon
1 tablespoon toasted hazelnuts
1 tablespoon olive oil
100 g (3½ oz) haloumi cheese, cut into 8 slices
150 g (5 oz) bulgar wheat
2 cooked beetroot, thinly sliced
65 g (2½ oz) mixed salad leaves
grated rind and juice of 1 orange
2 teaspoons clear honey
1 teaspoon Dijon mustard

preparation: 15 minutes, plus standing and cooling
cooking: 10 minutes
serves: 4

nutritional values per serving
Kcals: 297 (1240 kj)
Protein: 11 g
Carb: 37 g
Fat: 13 g

1 Place the herbs, lemon rind and juice, hazelnuts and oil in a food processor or blender and process until almost smooth but retaining a little texture. Pour over the haloumi slices and set aside for 10 minutes.

2 Heat a griddle until hot. Lay the marinated haloumi slices on the griddle and cook for 1–2 minutes on each side until beginning to brown.

3 Prepare the bulgar wheat according to the pack instructions. Leave to cool, then stir through the beetroot and salad leaves. In a small bowl whisk together the orange rind and juice, honey and mustard, then drizzle over the bulgar and stir to combine. Serve the salad topped with the haloumi.

nutritional tip
Beetroot is packed full of useful vitamins and minerals, including vitamin B6, iron, calcium and potassium. It can help you fight off infection and has also been credited as a possible anti-cancer food.

Chicken and vegetable salad with a peanut dressing

400 g (13 oz) carrots, coarsely grated
400 g (13 oz) white or Savoy cabbage, shredded
2 lean boneless, skinless chicken breasts, cooked and sliced
100 g (3½ oz) bean sprouts
flour tortillas or pitta bread, to serve
dressing
4 tablespoons peanut butter
8 tablespoons coconut milk
1 fresh red chilli, finely chopped
2 tablespoons chopped fresh coriander

preparation: 15 minutes
serves: 4

nutritional values per serving
Kcals: 277 (1157 kj)
Protein: 25 g
Carb: 17 g
Fat: 12 g

1 In a large bowl mix together all the salad ingredients. In a small bowl whisk together all the dressing ingredients.

2 Drizzle the dressing over the salad and toss together. Serve the salad with flour tortillas or pitta bread to make a tasty wrap or sandwich.

Eggs baked with spinach and ham

175 g (6 oz) baby spinach leaves
1 tablespoon water
100 g (4 oz) sliced ham, chopped
1 tomato, sliced into 4
4 eggs
4 tablespoons light crème fraîche
40 g (1½ oz) mature Cheddar cheese, grated
salt (optional) and pepper
multigrain bread, to serve

preparation: 10 minutes
cooking: 15 minutes
serves: 4

nutritional values per serving
Kcals: 178 (740 kj)
Protein: 14 g
Carb: 2 g
Fat: 13 g

1 Place the spinach in a saucepan with the water and heat gently for 2–3 minutes until the spinach is wilted.

2 Divide the spinach among 4 mini pudding basins or dariole moulds, top with ham and a tomato slice, then break an egg into each. Spoon a tablespoon of crème fraîche over each, sprinkle with Cheddar and season with salt, if liked, and pepper.

3 Place the dishes on a baking sheet and bake in a preheated oven, 200°C (400°F), Gas Mark 6, for 10 minutes until the eggs are just set. Serve with multigrain bread to dip in the juices.

Blue cheese soufflés with chicory and walnut salad

25 g (1 oz) polyunsaturated margarine
50 g (2 oz) plain flour
300 ml (½ pint) milk
4 eggs, separated
100 g (3½ oz) Stilton cheese, crumbled
1 teaspoon chopped thyme
oil, for oiling
4 heads of chicory, leaves separated
handful of watercress
1 tablespoon walnuts, toasted
2 tablespoons fat-free dressing
pepper

preparation: 25 minutes
cooking: 10–12 minutes
serves: 4

nutritional values per serving
Kcals: 360 (1505 kj)
Protein: 18 g
Carb: 16 g
Fat: 26 g

1 Melt the margarine in a medium-sized saucepan, add the flour and stir over the heat for 1 minute. Gradually add the milk, whisking constantly, and cook until thickened.

2 Remove the pan from the heat and beat in the egg yolks, one at a time. Stir in the Stilton and thyme and season well with pepper. In a large, clean bowl whisk the egg whites until they form firm peaks. Gradually fold them into the cheese mixture.

3 Transfer the mixture to 4 lightly oiled ramekins and bake in a preheated oven, 190°C (375°F), Gas Mark 5, for 10–12 minutes until risen and golden. Toss the remaining ingredients together and serve with the soufflés.

nutritional tip
Walnuts are a great source of potassium and vitamin E, as well as being rich in beneficial omega-3 and omega-6 oils. Store them in the refrigerator or in a cool, dry place in an airtight container to keep fresh.

New potato, watercress and bacon salad

900 g (1 lb 13 oz) baby new potatoes, scrubbed
4 lean back bacon rashers, chopped
2 tablespoons olive oil
1 teaspoon Dijon mustard
4 tablespoons lemon juice
1 teaspoon clear honey
150 g (5 oz) watercress, roughly chopped
2 heads of red chicory or radicchio, cut into bite-sized pieces
pepper

preparation: 10 minutes, plus standing
cooking: 20 minutes
serves: 4

nutritional values per serving
Kcals: 260 (1096 kj)
Protein: 10 g
Carb: 39 g
Fat: 9 g

1 Cook the potatoes in a saucepan of boiling water for 12–15 minutes until tender. Drain and tip into a serving bowl.

2 Cook the bacon in a dry, nonstick pan for 3–4 minutes until crisp. Add the oil, mustard, lemon juice and honey and stir well. Tip into the bowl with the potatoes, mix together and set aside for 30 minutes. Stir through the remaining ingredients and season well with pepper. Serve.

Turkey and avocado salad with toasted seeds

450 g (14½ oz) cooked turkey, sliced
1 large avocado, sliced
2 red apples, cored and sliced
1 punnet of mustard cress
125 g (4 oz) mixed salad leaves
50 g (2 oz) toasted mixed seeds (such as pumpkin and sunflower)
wholegrain rye bread, to serve

dressing

3 tablespoons apple juice
3 tablespoons low-fat natural yogurt
1 teaspoon clear honey
1 teaspoon wholegrain mustard

preparation: 10 minutes
serves: 4

nutritional values per serving
Kcals: 372 (1557 kj)
Protein: 39 g
Carb: 15 g
Fat: 18 g

1 In a large bowl toss together all the salad ingredients. In a separate bowl whisk together all the dressing ingredients.

2 Pour the dressing over the salad, mix together well and serve with slices of wholegrain rye bread.

Bulgar wheat salad with fennel, orange and spinach

150 g (5 oz) bulgar wheat
2 tablespoons olive oil
2 fennel bulbs, finely sliced
175 g (6 oz) baby spinach leaves
3 oranges, segmented
2 tablespoons pumpkin seeds, toasted

dressing

4 tablespoons natural yogurt
2 tablespoons chopped fresh coriander
½ small cucumber, finely chopped
salt (optional) and pepper

preparation: 10 minutes, plus cooling
cooking: 15 minutes
serves: 4

nutritional values per serving
Kcals: 296 (1237 kj)
Protein: 10 g
Carb: 44 g
Fat: 9 g

1 Prepare the bulgar wheat according to the pack instructions. Set aside to cool. Heat half the oil in a frying pan, add the fennel and fry for 8–10 minutes until tender and browned. Add the spinach to the pan and stir through until just wilted.

2 Toss the spinach through the bulgar wheat, then the orange segments and pumpkin seeds. Mix together all the dressing ingredients with the remaining oil, stir through the salad and serve.

Low-fat chicken Caesar salad

4 small boneless, skinless chicken breasts
1 tablespoon olive oil
2 cos lettuces, chopped
½ cucumber, sliced
croûtons
4 slices of wholegrain bread
1 garlic clove, halved
dressing
3 tablespoons light crème fraîche
1 anchovy fillet, chopped
grated rind and juice of ½ lemon
2 tablespoons freshly grated Parmesan cheese
salt (optional) and pepper

preparation: 15 minutes
cooking: 10 minutes
serves: 4

nutritional values per serving
Kcals: 279 (1170 kj)
Protein: 28 g
Carb: 18 g
Fat: 11 g

1 Brush the chicken breasts with a little of the oil and season well with pepper. Heat a griddle until hot, lay on the chicken breasts and cook for 3–4 minutes on each side until cooked through. Slice each chicken breast.

2 Divide the lettuce and cucumber among 4 serving plates and top each with a sliced chicken breast.

3 To make the croûtons, drizzle the remaining oil over the bread and grill until toasted on each side. Rub all over with the cut sides of the garlic, cut the toast into cubes and add to the salad.

4 Blend together all the dressing ingredients and drizzle over the salad. Serve.

Tortilla pizza

4 medium flour tortillas
4 tomatoes, thinly sliced
2 pears, peeled, cored and thinly sliced
100 g (3½ oz) Gorgonzola cheese, or other blue cheese, crumbled
4 tablespoons light crème fraîche
65 g (2½ oz) rocket
pepper

preparation: 10 minutes
cooking: 10 minutes
serves: 4

nutritional values per serving
Kcals: 274 (1150 kj)
Protein: 10 g
Carb: 35 g
Fat: 11 g

1 Place the tortillas on a baking sheet (or 2 sheets if needed). Layer the tomatoes, pears and Gorgonzola over the tortillas, spoon over the crème fraîche and season with pepper.

2 Cook the tortillas in a preheated oven, 220°C (425°F), Gas Mark 7, for 10 minutes until the cheese is bubbling. Scatter over the rocket and serve.

Homemade hummus with roasted vegetables in tortillas

400 g (13 oz) can chickpeas, rinsed and drained
1 garlic clove
2 tablespoons Greek yogurt
4 tablespoons lemon juice
pinch of paprika
1 aubergine, cut into batons
1 red pepper, cored, deseeded and sliced
2 courgettes, sliced
2 carrots, cut into batons
1 red onion, sliced
1 tablespoon olive oil
1 teaspoon chopped thyme
8 small flour tortillas

preparation: 10 minutes
cooking: 45 minutes
serves: 4

nutritional values per serving
Kcals: 422 (1783 kj)
Protein: 16 g
Carb: 74 g
Fat: 9 g

1 Place the chickpeas, garlic, yogurt, lemon juice and paprika in a food processor or blender and process until smooth. Tip into a bowl, cover and set aside.

2 Place the prepared vegetables in a roasting tin, drizzle over the oil and sprinkle over the thyme. Cook in a preheated oven, 200°C (400°F), Gas Mark 6, for 45 minutes until tender and beginning to char.

3 Meanwhile, warm the tortillas according to the pack instructions, fill with the roasted vegetables and the hummus and serve.

nutritional tip

High in fibre and protein, chickpeas, along with lentils and other legumes, are particularly beneficial to a vegetarian diet. However, as the fibre they contain can also help reduce cholesterol, we should all be eating more of them.

Poached eggs with lentils and rocket

250 g (8 oz) Puy lentils
450 ml (¾ pint) vegetable stock
1 teaspoon olive oil
4 spring onions, finely sliced
3 tomatoes, chopped
125 g (4 oz) rocket
4 eggs
salt (optional) and pepper

preparation: 10 minutes
cooking: 1 hour
serves: 4

nutritional values per serving
Kcals: 304 (1284 kj)
Protein: 24 g
Carb: 33 g
Fat: 10 g

1 Place the lentils and stock in a medium-sized saucepan and bring to the boil. Reduce the heat and simmer for about 40 minutes until tender. Drain off any excess liquid.

2 Heat the oil in a frying pan, add the spring onions and tomatoes and fry for 2 minutes. Stir through the lentils and rocket and season with salt, if liked, and pepper.

3 Bring a large saucepan of lightly salted water to the boil, then reduce to a very gentle simmer and crack in one of the eggs. Swirl the water very gently to wrap the white around the yolk and cook for 3 minutes. Remove the egg from the pan and repeat with the remaining eggs. Serve on top of the lentils and rocket.

Creamy mushroom medley on toast

1 tablespoon olive oil

1 garlic clove, crushed (optional)

750 g (1½ lb) mixed mushrooms (such as flat cap, oyster and cep), trimmed and sliced

1 tablespoon wholegrain mustard

2 tablespoons light crème fraîche

2 tablespoons chopped parsley

4 thick slices of Granary toast

preparation: 10 minutes
cooking: 10 minutes
serves: 4

nutritional values per serving
Kcals: 206 (869 kj)
Protein: 9 g
Carb: 27 g
Fat: 7 g

1 Heat the oil in a large frying pan, add the garlic, if liked, and fry for 1 minute. Add the mushrooms and sauté for 5–6 minutes until tender.

2 Stir the mustard, crème fraîche and parsley into the mushrooms and bring to the boil. Remove from the heat and serve on the Granary toast.

Spinach, butter bean and ricotta frittata

1 teaspoon olive oil
1 onion, sliced
400 g (13 oz) can butter beans, rinsed and drained
200 g (7 oz) baby spinach leaves
4 eggs, beaten
50 g (2 oz) ricotta cheese
salt (optional) and pepper
tomato and onion salad, to serve

preparation: 10 minutes
cooking: 10 minutes
serves: 2

nutritional values per serving
Kcals: 417 (1748 kj)
Protein: 32 g
Carb: 34 g
Fat: 18 g

1 Heat the oil in a medium-sized frying pan, add the onion and fry for 3–4 minutes until softened. Add the butter beans and spinach and heat gently for 2–3 minutes until the spinach has wilted.

2 Pour over the eggs, then spoon over the ricotta and season with salt, if liked, and pepper. Cook until almost set, then place under a hot grill and cook for 1–2 minutes until golden and set. Serve with a tomato and onion salad.

Sautéed chicken livers with wilted baby spinach

1 tablespoon olive oil
1 garlic clove, crushed
1 teaspoon chopped thyme
450 g (14½ oz) chicken livers
175 g (6 oz) baby spinach leaves
1 tablespoon balsamic vinegar
pepper
4 thick slices of Granary bread, toasted, to serve

preparation: 5 minutes
cooking: 10 minutes
serves: 4

nutritional values per serving
Kcals: 318 (1340 kj)
Protein: 28 g
Carb: 27 g
Fat: 12 g

1 Heat the oil in a medium-sized frying pan, add the garlic and fry for 1 minute. Add the thyme and chicken livers to the pan and fry for 2–3 minutes.

2 Stir in the spinach and balsamic vinegar and cook for 1–2 minutes until the spinach has wilted. Season with pepper and serve on Granary toast.

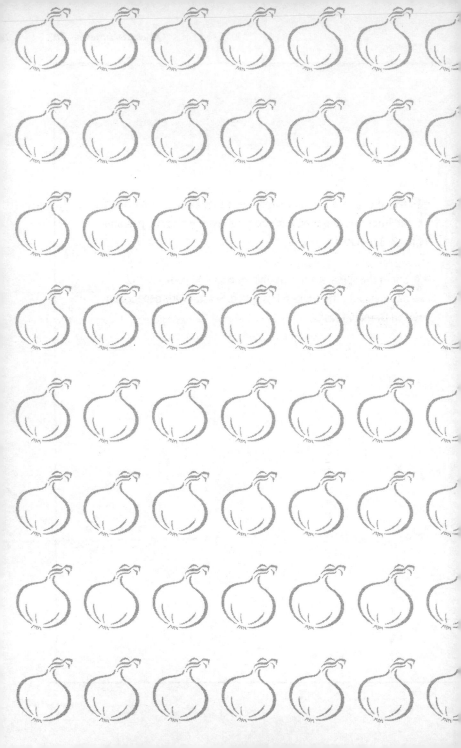

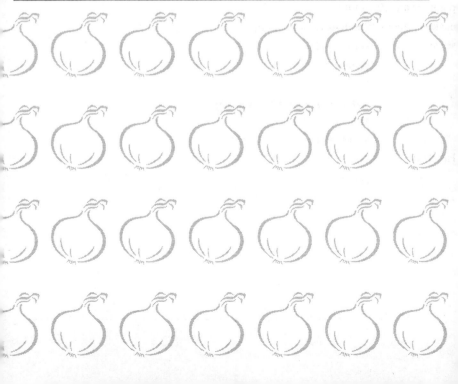

Delectable dinners

This range of recipes shows just how flexible following a low-GI eating plan really is. Whether it's quick after-work meals or something a bit special, look no further.

Lamb with braised lentils

4 lean lamb steaks
grated rind and juice of 1 lemon
1 tablespoon chopped rosemary
1 garlic clove, crushed
2 lean smoked back bacon rashers, chopped
2 onions, sliced
1 carrot, finely chopped
1 celery stick, finely chopped
250 g (8 oz) green or Puy lentils
450 ml (¾ pint) vegetable stock

preparation: 15 minutes
cooking: 40–50 minutes
serves: 4

nutritional values per serving
Kcals: 492 (2073 kj)
Protein: 50 g
Carb: 38 g
Fat: 17 g

1 Rub the lamb steaks with the lemon rind, rosemary and garlic, and squeeze over the lemon juice. Heat a large, nonstick frying pan until hot, add the lamb steaks and fry for 1 minute on each side.

2 Remove the lamb from the pan. Add the bacon, onions, carrot and celery to the pan and fry for 2–3 minutes until beginning to soften. Add the lentils and stock, then return the lamb to the pan and bring to the boil. Reduce the heat and simmer gently for 30–40 minutes until the lentils are tender and most of the stock is absorbed. Serve each lamb steak on a bed of lentils.

Braised lamb with fruity pilaf

4 lamb shanks, about 200 g (7 oz) each
12 small rosemary sprigs
4 garlic cloves, each cut into 3 slices
1 teaspoon olive oil
2 onions, cut into wedges
600 ml (1 pint) lamb or beef stock
200 g (7 oz) long grain rice
12 ready-to-eat dried apricots
4 dried figs, halved
pepper
seasonal vegetables, to serve

preparation: 10 minutes
cooking: 1¾ hours
serves: 4

nutritional values per serving
Kcals: 599 (2518 kj)
Protein: 39 g
Carb: 79 g
Fat: 15 g

1 Make 3 deep incisions in each lamb shank and insert a rosemary sprig and a piece of garlic into each incision. Season well with pepper.

2 Heat the oil in a large, flameproof casserole, add the lamb shanks and onions and fry for 4–5 minutes, turning, until browned all over. Pour over the stock and bring to the boil. Reduce the heat, cover the pan and simmer very gently for 1½ hours until the meat is tender.

3 Add the rice and fruit to the pan, cover and cook for 10–12 minutes until the stock is absorbed and the rice is cooked. Serve with seasonal vegetables.

nutritional tip
High in fibre and vitamin C, apricots are good for boosting your immune system and easing constipation. They also make a great snack.

Lemon grass chicken with wok-fried vegetables

18 lemon grass stalks
8 boneless, skinless chicken thighs
1 garlic clove
2 lime leaves
2 tablespoons soy sauce
1 teaspoon sesame oil
1 red pepper, cored, deseeded and sliced
1 green pepper, cored, deseeded and sliced
350 g (11½ oz) sugar snap peas
2 pak choi, quartered lengthways

preparation: 15 minutes, plus soaking
cooking: about 10 minutes
serves: 4

nutritional values per serving
Kcals: 190 (805 kj)
Protein: 25 g
Carb: 9 g
Fat: 7 g

1 Place 16 of the lemon grass stalks in a bowl of water and leave to soak for 1 hour. Chop the remaining 2 stalks.

2 Place the chicken, chopped lemon grass, garlic, lime leaves and half the soy sauce in a food processor and process until well combined. Divide the mixture into 16 portions and mould each portion around a piece of the soaked lemon grass.

3 Place the skewers on a baking sheet, drizzle with half the oil and cook under a hot grill for 4–5 minutes, turning occasionally, until golden and cooked through.

4 Heat the remaining oil in a wok or frying pan, add the vegetables and stir-fry for 2–3 minutes until just tender, then add the remaining soy sauce. Serve the stir-fried vegetables with the chicken.

Stuffed chicken with sautéed greens and seeds

4 large boneless, skinless chicken thighs
75 g (3 oz) mozzarella cheese, cut into 4 slices
25 g (1 oz) toasted walnuts, chopped
2 tablespoons chopped parsley
8 ready-to-eat dried apricots, chopped
2 teaspoons olive oil
50 g (2 oz) pancetta, finely chopped
1 Savoy cabbage, shredded
25 g (1 oz) mixed seeds (such as pumpkin, sesame and sunflower)

preparation: 10 minutes
cooking: 30 minutes
serves: 4

nutritional values per serving
Kcals: 350 (1467 kj)
Protein: 28 g
Carb: 20 g
Fat: 18 g

1 Open out the chicken thighs, then beat a little to flatten slightly. Lay a piece of mozzarella on each chicken piece. Mix together the walnuts, parsley and apricots and divide among the chicken pieces. Roll up each chicken piece and secure with a cocktail stick.

2 Heat half the oil in a nonstick frying pan, add the chicken and fry for 2–3 minutes, turning, until browned all over. Place the chicken on a baking sheet and bake in a preheated oven, 200°C (400°F), Gas Mark 6, for 20 minutes until cooked through and the cheese begins to ooze.

3 Meanwhile, heat the remaining oil in a pan. Add the pancetta and fry for 2 minutes, then add the cabbage and mixed seeds and continue to fry for 5 minutes until the cabbage is tender. Serve with the chicken.

Baked sweet potato with griddled herb chicken

4 sweet potatoes, about 250 g (8 oz) each
4 boneless, skinless chicken breasts
6 tablespoons mixed herbs (such as mint, parsley, fresh coriander
   and oregano)
1 garlic clove
1 tablespoon capers
2 teaspoons clear honey
1 tablespoon Dijon mustard
1 tablespoon olive oil
4 tablespoons light cream cheese
pepper

preparation: 10 minutes, plus marinating
cooking: about 1½ hours
serves: 4

nutritional values per serving
Kcals: 435 (1842 kj)
Protein: 34 g
Carb: 52 g
Fat: 12 g

1 Place the potatoes on a baking sheet and cook in a preheated oven, 200°C (400°F), Gas Mark 6, for 1–1¼ hours until tender.

2 Meanwhile, make 3 incisions in the flesh of the chicken (be careful you don't cut all the way through). Place the herbs, garlic, capers, honey, mustard and a little of the oil in a food processor or blender and process until well combined. Rub this mixture over the chicken, cover and leave in the refrigerator for at least 30 minutes for the flavours to develop.

3 Heat a griddle until hot, drizzle the remaining oil over the chicken, then place the chicken on the griddle and cook for 3–4 minutes on each side until beginning to char and the chicken is cooked through.

4 Cut open the sweet potatoes, spoon in some cream cheese and season with plenty of pepper. Serve with the chicken.

Griddled duck with plum confit and layered potatoes

450 g (14½ oz) new potatoes, scrubbed and thinly sliced
2 garlic cloves, thinly sliced
1 teaspoon chopped thyme
2 tablespoons olive oil
150 ml (¼ pint) water
4 boneless, skinless duck breasts
4 teaspoons Chinese five-spice powder
2 large onions, sliced
1 tablespoon sugar
2 tablespoons white wine vinegar
6 plums, halved, stoned and sliced
pepper
steamed green vegetables, to serve

preparation: 15 minutes
cooking: 1 hour
serves: 4

nutritional values per serving
Kcals: 375 (1575 kj)
Protein: 30 g
Carb: 39 g
Fat: 12 g

1 Layer the potatoes, garlic and thyme in a shallow, ovenproof dish. Mix together half the oil and the water, pour over the potatoes and season well with pepper. Cover with foil and cook in a preheated oven, 180°C (350°F), Gas Mark 4, for 1 hour until the potatoes are tender, removing the foil halfway through cooking.

2 Meanwhile, rub the duck with the five-spice powder, place on a hot griddle or in a hot frying pan and fry for 3–4 minutes on each side, draining off any excess fat. Keep the duck warm.

3 Heat the remaining oil in a small saucepan, add the onions and sugar and fry for 10 minutes until caramelized. Add the vinegar and plums, season with pepper and continue to cook for a further 10 minutes.

4 Slice the duck and serve with the potatoes and plum confit, and plenty of green vegetables.

Bolognese-filled pasta shells with cheeses

1 teaspoon olive oil

1 onion, chopped

1 celery stick, chopped

1 carrot, chopped

200 g (7 oz) mushrooms, sliced

450 g (14½ oz) turkey mince

300 ml (½ pint) passata

2 tablespoons chopped parsley

16 large wholewheat pasta shells, cooked according to pack instructions

100 g (3½ oz) ricotta cheese

2 tablespoons freshly grated Parmesan cheese

pepper

salad, to serve

preparation: 15 minutes

cooking: 40 minutes

serves: 4

nutritional values per serving

Kcals: 515 (2189 kj)

Protein 43 g

Carb: 68 g

Fat: 10 g

1 Heat the oil in a large frying pan, add the onion, celery, carrot and mushrooms and fry for 3–4 minutes until softened.

2 Add the turkey mince and continue to fry, stirring to break up, for 5 minutes until browned. Pour the passata over the mince and bring to the boil. Reduce the heat and simmer for 20 minutes. Stir through the parsley and season well with pepper.

3 Place the cooked pasta shells in a large, ovenproof dish and divide the Bolognese mixture among them. Spoon a little ricotta on top of each, then sprinkle over the Parmesan. Bake in a preheated oven, 200°C (400°F), Gas Mark 6, for 10 minutes until golden and bubbling. Serve with a salad.

Gourmet 'Greek' burgers

450 g (14½ oz) steak mince
1 tablespoon sun-dried tomato paste
2 teaspoons chopped oregano
50 g (2 oz) feta cheese, crumbled
a little beaten egg
4 wholemeal rolls, toasted
1 red onion, sliced
1 Little Gem lettuce, leaves separated
pepper

preparation: 10 minutes
cooking: about 10 minutes
serves: 4

nutritional values per serving
Kcals: 324 (1364 kj)
Protein: 30 g
Carb: 27 g
Fat: 11 g

1 In a large bowl, mix together the steak mince, tomato paste, oregano and feta. Season well with pepper and stir through enough beaten egg to bind. Form the mixture into 4 burgers.

2 Place the burgers under a hot grill and cook for 4–5 minutes on each side until browned and cooked through. Make up the burgers in the rolls with the onion and lettuce and serve with a napkin.

Spice-encrusted beef fillet with haricot bean mash

1 teaspoon coriander seeds
1 teaspoon cumin seeds
1 teaspoon mixed peppercorns
4 fillet steaks, about 125 g (4 oz) each
1 teaspoon olive oil
2 x 400 g (13 oz) cans haricot beans, rinsed and drained
200 ml (7 fl oz) vegetable stock
2 tablespoons light crème fraîche
2 tablespoons chopped fresh coriander

preparation: 10 minutes
cooking: about 15 minutes
serves: 4

nutritional values per serving
Kcals: 349 (1473 kj)
Protein: 37 g
Carb: 27 g
Fat: 11 g

1 Place the spices in a dry frying pan and fry for 1 minute, then transfer to a mortar and roughly crush with a pestle.

2 Press the steak into the spices to cover all over. Heat the oil in the pan, add the steaks and cook for 3 minutes on each side, or until cooked to your liking.

3 Meanwhile, place the haricot beans and stock in a saucepan and bring to the boil. Reduce the heat and simmer for 10 minutes, then drain. Very lightly mash the beans together with the remaining ingredients and serve with the steak.

Sticky pork steaks with pearl barley salad

4 lean pork steaks, about 150 g (5 oz) each
2 tablespoons tomato ketchup
1 tablespoon clear honey
1 teaspoon fennel seeds
1 garlic clove, crushed
2 teaspoons Worcestershire sauce
grated rind and juice of 1 orange
200 g (7 oz) pearl barley, prepared and cooked according to pack instructions
seeds of 1 pomegranate
4 spring onions, sliced
2 tablespoons chopped mint
200 g (7 oz) cherry tomatoes, quartered
1 tablespoon olive oil

preparation: 15 minutes, plus marinating
cooking: 20-25 minutes
serves: 4

nutritional values per serving
Kcals: 476 (2010 kj)
Protein: 36 g
Carb: 54 g
Fat: 15 g

1 Place the pork steaks in an ovenproof dish. Mix together the ketchup, honey, fennel seeds, garlic, Worcestershire sauce and orange rind and pour over the steaks. Turn to coat in the sauce, then cover and leave in the refrigerator for 30 minutes.

2 Drain the pearl barley, then toss through the pomegranate seeds, onions, mint, tomatoes, orange juice and oil. Cover and set aside.

3 Place the pork in a preheated oven, 220°C (425°F), Gas Mark 7, and cook for 20–25 minutes until cooked and the sauce is sticky. Serve with the salad, pouring over any excess sauce.

Chilli prawns with lime basmati

450 g (14½ oz) raw tiger prawns, peeled
2 garlic cloves, crushed
2 fresh red chillies, finely chopped
2 tablespoons chopped fresh coriander
1 teaspoon sesame oil
grated rind and juice of 2 limes (reserve 2 of the lime 'shells')
225 g (7½ oz) basmati rice, rinsed
350 ml (12 fl oz) boiling water
25 g (1 oz) creamed coconut
4 tablespoons water
25 g (1 oz) peanuts, crushed, to garnish (optional)

preparation: 15 minutes
cooking: 20 minutes
serves: 4

nutritional values per serving
Kcals: 367 (1535 kj)
Protein: 26 g
Carb: 48 g
Fat: 7 g

1 Place the prawns in a non-metallic bowl. Place the garlic, chillies, coriander, oil and half the lime rind and juice in a mortar and grind with a pestle to make a paste or use a food processor or blender. Tip over the prawns and stir so that the prawns are coated with the paste.

2 Place the rice in a saucepan and pour over the boiling water, the lime 'shells' and the remaining lime rind and juice. Bring to the boil, reduce the heat, cover and simmer for 12–15 minutes until the liquid is absorbed and the rice is tender and fluffy.

3 Meanwhile, heat a dry frying pan until hot, then add the prawns and paste and fry for 2–3 minutes until they just turn pink. Add the coconut and water and bring to the boil, then reduce the heat and simmer for 1 minute. Serve the prawns with the rice, sprinkling over the peanuts to garnish, if liked.

nutritional tip

When you are choosing chillies, there's a general rule to follow: the smaller the chilli, the hotter the flavour. But with their high vitamin C content and antibacterial properties, you should definitely turn up the heat.

Fragrant prawn curry

6 spring onions, chopped
1–2 fresh green chillies, halved
2 garlic cloves, crushed
2 teaspoons rapeseed oil
1 teaspoon turmeric
1 teaspoon cumin seeds
1 teaspoon ground cumin
1 teaspoon mustard seeds
1 teaspoon ground coriander
5 tomatoes, chopped
2 tablespoons water
4 tablespoons double cream
50 g (2 oz) creamed coconut, dissolved in 100 ml (3½ fl oz) boiling
    water
450 g (14½ oz) cooked peeled prawns
2 tablespoons chopped fresh coriander
flat bread or boiled rice, to serve

preparation: 15 minutes
cooking: 15 minutes
serves: 4

nutritional values per serving
Kcals: 387 (1608 kj)
Protein: 28 g
Carb: 7 g
Fat: 27 g

1 Place the spring onions, chillies and garlic in a mortar and grind with a pestle to make a paste or use a food processor or blender.

2 Heat the oil in a saucepan, add the turmeric, cumin seeds, ground cumin, mustard seeds and ground coriander and fry for 1 minute. Add the spring onion paste and fry for 2–3 minutes.

3 Add the tomatoes and water to the pan and simmer for 5 minutes. Add the double cream and creamed coconut and simmer for a further 2 minutes. Stir in the prawns and fresh coriander, heat through and serve with flat bread or rice.

Spaghetti with crab and lemon sauce

350 g (11½ oz) spaghetti
1 teaspoon olive oil
bunch of spring onions, sliced
2 garlic cloves, crushed
1 fresh red chilli, finely sliced
300 g (10 oz) cooked fresh white crab meat
grated rind and juice of 1 lemon
6 tablespoons light crème fraîche
salt (optional) and pepper
salad, to serve

preparation: 10 minutes
cooking: about 10 minutes
serves: 4

nutritional values per serving
Kcals: 459 (1944 kj)
Protein: 27 g
Carb: 68 g
Fat: 11 g

1 Cook the spaghetti in a large saucepan of boiling water according to the pack instructions. Drain well.

2 Heat the oil in a large frying pan, then add the spring onions, garlic and chilli and fry for 3 minutes. Add the remaining ingredients with the cooked pasta. Season with salt, if liked, and pepper and heat through. Serve with a salad.

Smoked haddock and pea risotto

1 teaspoon olive oil
1 small onion, finely chopped
350 g (11½ oz) arborio rice
1 small glass dry white wine
900 ml (1½ pints) vegetable stock, boiling
350 g (11½ oz) smoked haddock fillet, skinned and cubed
200 g (7 oz) frozen peas
2 tablespoons chopped chives
3 tablespoons freshly grated Parmesan cheese, plus extra to serve
   (optional)
pepper
green salad, to serve

preparation: 10 minutes
cooking: 25 minutes
serves: 4

nutritional values per serving
Kcals: 496 (2100 kj)
Protein: 27 g
Carb: 82 g
Fat: 7 g

1 Heat the oil in a large, nonstick frying pan, add the onion and fry for 2–3 minutes until beginning to soften. Stir in the rice, coating it in the oil, then pour in the wine and allow to absorb.

2 Add the stock, a ladleful at a time, allowing each amount to be absorbed before adding the next. Stir constantly. Add the haddock and peas with the last ladleful of stock and cook for a further 5 minutes until the fish flakes easily.

3 Stir in the remaining ingredients and season well with pepper. The process will take about 20 minutes. Serve with a green salad and extra grated Parmesan, if liked.

Baked salmon parcels

4 pieces of skinless salmon fillet, about 125 g (4 oz) each
1 orange, cut into 8 slices
4 spring onions, shredded
4 tablespoons light crème fraîche
handful of basil leaves
salt (optional) and pepper
to serve
boiled new potatoes
salad or steamed vegetables

preparation: 15 minutes
cooking: 10–12 minutes
serves: 4

nutritional values per serving
Kcals: 287 (1196 kj)
Protein: 25 g
Carb: 5 g
Fat: 19 g

1 Place each piece of salmon in the centre of a 25 cm (10 inch) square of foil and top each with 2 orange slices. Mix together the remaining ingredients and divide among the salmon fillets.

2 Fold up each square of foil securely to enclose the salmon. Place the parcels on a baking sheet and bake in a preheated oven, 200°C (400°F), Gas Mark 6, for 10–12 minutes. Serve the salmon with new potatoes and a salad or vegetables.

Linguine with rocket pesto and goats' cheese

350 g (11½ oz) linguine (or a pasta shape of your choice)
125 g (4 oz) rocket
40 g (1½ oz) toasted hazelnuts
40 g (1½ oz) Parmesan cheese, freshly grated
3 tablespoons natural yogurt
100 g (3½ oz) goats' cheese, chopped
pepper

preparation: 10 minutes
cooking: about 10 minutes
serves: 4

nutritional values per serving
Kcals: 484 (2039 kj)
Protein: 22 g
Carb: 68 g
Fat: 16 g

1 Cook the pasta in a large saucepan of boiling water according to the pack instructions. Drain well.

2 Meanwhile, place the rocket, hazelnuts, Parmesan and yogurt in a food processor or blender and process until almost smooth. Toss the mixture through the pasta with the goats' cheese, to warm through, season well with pepper and serve.

Asian-marinated salmon with stir-fried rice noodles

4 pieces of salmon fillet, about 125 g (4 oz) each
1 garlic clove, crushed
2.5 cm (1 inch) piece of fresh root ginger, peeled and grated
2 tablespoons soy sauce
2 tablespoons rice wine vinegar
1 tablespoon sesame oil
250 g (8 oz) medium rice noodles
200 g (7 oz) mangetout, halved lengthways
150 g (5 oz) shiitake mushrooms, trimmed and sliced
4 spring onions, sliced
100 g (3½ oz) bean sprouts
2 pak choi, quartered lengthways

preparation: 15 minutes, plus marinating
cooking: about 10 minutes
serves: 4

nutritional values per serving
Kcals: 528 (2206 kj)
Protein: 32 g
Carb: 58 g
Fat: 18 g

1 Place the salmon in a non-metallic dish. Whisk together the garlic, ginger, soy sauce, vinegar and half the oil. Pour over the salmon, cover and set aside in a cool place for at least 10 minutes to allow the flavours to develop.

2 Heat a griddle or a nonstick frying pan until hot, add the salmon, reserving the marinade, and cook for 2–3 minutes on each side until just cooked through. Meanwhile, cook the noodles according to the pack instructions and drain.

3 Heat the remaining oil in a frying pan or wok, add the mangetout, mushrooms, spring onions, bean sprouts and pak choi and stir-fry for 3–4 minutes. Add the reserved marinade and the noodles to the pan, toss together and heat through. Serve topped with a piece of salmon.

Tofu and tomato pasta

350 g (11½ oz) wholewheat pasta shapes
1 tablespoon olive oil
250 g (8 oz) firm tofu, cut into bite-sized cubes
6 spring onions, sliced
450 g (14½ oz) cherry tomatoes, halved
handful of basil, torn
1 garlic clove, crushed
salt (optional) and pepper

preparation: 10 minutes
cooking: 15 minutes
serves: 4

nutritional values per serving
Kcals: 378 (1600 kj)
Protein: 18 g
Carb: 63 g
Fat: 8 g

1 Cook the pasta in a large saucepan of boiling water according to the pack instructions. Drain well.

2 Meanwhile, heat the oil in a nonstick frying pan, add the tofu and fry for 3–4 minutes until golden. Mix together the remaining ingredients and toss through the pasta with the tofu. Season with salt, if liked, and pepper and serve.

Moroccan vegetable stew

2 teaspoons olive oil
2 garlic cloves, sliced
2 onions, sliced
1 aubergine, chopped
625 g (1¼ lb) sweet potatoes, chopped
1 teaspoon ground cumin
1 teaspoon ground coriander
½ teaspoon turmeric
600 ml (1 pint) vegetable stock
200 g (7 oz) green beans
400 g (13 oz) can chickpeas, rinsed and drained
4 tomatoes, chopped
350 g (11½ oz) couscous
2 tablespoons chopped mixed herbs (such as mint, parsley and
    fresh coriander)
grated rind and juice of 1 lemon

preparation: 20 minutes
cooking: 25 minutes
serves: 4

nutritional values per serving
Kcals: 529 (2234 kj)
Protein: 17 g
Carb: 106 g
Fat: 7 g

1 Heat the oil in a medium-sized saucepan. Add the garlic and onions and fry for 2-3 minutes until beginning to soften. Add the aubergine and sweet potatoes and fry for 3-4 minutes, then add the spices and cook for 1 minute.

2 Pour the stock into the pan and bring to the boil. Reduce the heat and simmer for 10 minutes. Add the beans, chickpeas and tomatoes and simmer for a further 5 minutes.

3 Meanwhile, prepare the couscous according to the pack instructions. Mix the herbs into the couscous with the lemon rind and juice. Serve the couscous with the stew.

Stuffed roasted peppers on herby bulgar wheat

2 red peppers, halved, cored and deseeded
2 yellow or orange peppers, halved, cored and deseeded
16 cherry tomatoes, halved
4 tablespoons cream cheese or light crème fraîche
2 tablespoons pesto
125 g (4 oz) bulgar wheat
grated rind and juice of 1 lemon
4 tablespoons chopped mixed herbs (such as parsley, mint and
    oregano)
6 spring onions, sliced
2 tablespoons pine nuts
salt and pepper

preparation: 15 minutes
cooking: 30 minutes
serves: 4

nutritional values per serving
Kcals: 309 (1290 kj)
Protein: 11 g
Carb: 36 g
Fat: 14 g

1 Place the pepper halves on a baking sheet, cut side up. Divide the halved tomatoes among the peppers. Beat together the cream cheese or crème fraîche and pesto and spoon over the peppers.

2 Season the peppers well, then cook in a preheated oven, 200°C (400°F), Gas Mark 6, for 30 minutes until tender.

3 Meanwhile, prepare the bulgar wheat according to the pack instructions, then stir through the lemon rind and juice, herbs and spring onions. Lightly toast the pine nuts in a dry frying pan.

4 Serve the bulgar wheat with the peppers, sprinkled with the toasted pine nuts.

nutritional tip

Improved blood circulation, a strong immune system and protection against strokes, heart disease and certain cancers: these are just some of the health benefits you could enjoy by eating peppers.

Sweet treats

If you've got a sweet tooth, don't despair – low GI is about eating sensibly while also enjoying your food. We all need a little indulgence every now and again.

Plum tatin

50 g (2 oz) butter or polyunsaturated margarine
50 g (2 oz) golden caster sugar
600 g (1 lb 3 oz) plums (any variety), quartered and stoned
250 g (8 oz) ready-made shortcrust pastry
light crème fraîche or ice cream, to serve

preparation: 15 minutes, plus cooling
cooking: about 45 minutes
serves: 8

nutritional values per serving
Kcals: 222 (928 kj)
Protein: 2 g
Carb: 27 g
Fat: 12 g

1 Place the butter or margarine and sugar in a 22 cm (8½ inch) fixed-base cake tin over a medium heat and cook, stirring constantly, for about 5 minutes until golden.

2 Carefully arrange the plums in the tin, skin side down. Roll out the pastry to fit snugly over the top of the fruit and press down carefully.

3 Bake the tart in a preheated oven, 190°C (375°F), Gas Mark 5, for about 40 minutes until the pastry is golden and the juices are bubbling. Cool in the tin for 10 minutes, then invert on to a large plate and serve with a little crème fraîche or ice cream.

---

tip
You could use pastry made with half wholemeal flour if you prefer, giving a pastry with a lower GI.

Baked exotic fruit parcels with spiced cream

1 pineapple, prepared and cut into chunks
1 mango, peeled, stoned and chopped
2 bananas, chopped
250 g (8 oz) strawberries, halved
425 g (14 oz) can lychees, drained, a little juice reserved
2 pieces of preserved ginger, finely chopped
1 teaspoon mixed spice
4 tablespoons light crème fraîche

preparation: 15 minutes
cooking: 15 minutes
serves: 4

nutritional values per serving
Kcals: 230 (974 kj)
Protein: 3 g
Carb: 48 g
Fat: 4 g

1 Cut 4 x 25 cm (10 inch) squares of foil. Divide the fruit among the squares, add half the ginger and drizzle over a little of the reserved lychee juice. Fold up each square of foil securely to enclose the fruit.

2 Place the parcels on a baking sheet and cook in a preheated oven, 200°C (400°F), Gas Mark 6, for 15 minutes. Mix together the mixed spice, crème fraîche and remaining ginger and serve on the hot fruit parcels.

Baked gooseberries with oaty topping

750 g (1½ lb) fresh gooseberries, topped and tailed
2 tablespoons demerara sugar
4 tablespoons mascarpone cheese
25 g (1 oz) butter or polyunsaturated margarine, melted
2 tablespoons clear honey
175 g (6 oz) jumbo oats
50 g (2 oz) chopped mixed nuts
low-fat natural yogurt, to serve

preparation: 10 minutes
cooking: 35 minutes
serves: 4

nutritional values per serving
Kcals: 475 (1990 kj)
Protein: 10 g
Carb: 51 g
Fat: 27 g

1 Place the gooseberries in an ovenproof dish, sprinkle over the sugar and bake in a preheated oven, 200°C (400°F), Gas Mark 6, for 20 minutes until they are tender and oozing juice.

2 Spoon the mascarpone over the gooseberries. Mix together the remaining ingredients and spoon over the mascarpone. Return to the oven and bake for 15 minutes. Serve with natural yogurt.

---

tip

If fresh gooseberries are unavailable you can substitute the same quantity of fresh plums or rhubarb in the recipe.

Cappuccino panna cotta

300 ml (½ pint) semi-skimmed milk
50 g (2 oz) caster sugar
4 tablespoons double cream
½ teaspoon vanilla extract
2 gelatine leaves
150 g (5 oz) natural yogurt
4 tablespoons very strong cold black coffee
fresh raspberries, to serve

preparation: 10 minutes, plus cooling and chilling
cooking: 5 minutes
serves: 4

nutritional values per serving
Kcals: 247 (1029 kj)
Protein: 7 g
Carb: 21 g
Fat: 16 g

1 Pour the milk into a medium-sized saucepan with the sugar, cream and vanilla extract. Bring to the boil, then remove from the heat. Soak the gelatine leaves in cold water until soft.

2 Squeeze the water from the gelatine, then stir into the milk mixture until dissolved. Leave to cool (about 15 minutes) and then stir through the yogurt and coffee and whisk until smooth.

3 Strain, then pour the mixture into 4 dariole moulds. Chill in the refrigerator for 4–6 hours until set. Remove the panna cotta from the moulds by dipping the outside of each mould into a bowl of hot water for a couple of seconds, then tip on to serving plates. Serve with fresh raspberries.

Instant mixed berry frozen yogurt

450 g (14½ oz) mixed frozen summer berries (such as strawberries, raspberries and blackberries)
450 ml (¾ pint) light Greek yogurt
1 tablespoon icing sugar

preparation: 5 minutes
serves: 4

nutritional values per serving
Kcals: 129 (544 kj)
Protein: 7 g
Carb: 98 g
Fat: 3 g

Place all the ingredients in a food processor or blender and process until smooth. Serve immediately or store in a freezerproof container in the freezer until required.

Grapefruit syllabub

200 ml (7 fl oz) whipping cream
2 tablespoons caster sugar
200 ml (7 fl oz) light Greek yogurt
grated rind and juice of 1 grapefruit
1 grapefruit, segmented

preparation: 10 minutes
serves: 4

nutritional values per serving
Kcals: 272 (1130 kj)
Protein: 4 g
Carb: 53 g
Fat: 21 g

1 In a large bowl whip the cream with the sugar until it forms soft peaks. Fold through the yogurt and grapefruit rind and juice.

2 Divide the grapefruit segments among 4 tall glasses, then spoon over the syllabub. Serve immediately or chill in the refrigerator until required.

Blackberry and apple tartlets

175 g (6 oz) puff pastry, thawed if frozen
1 dessert apple, peeled, cored and very thinly sliced
a little melted butter, for brushing
200 g (7 oz) blackberries
2 tablespoons apricot jam, warmed
yogurt or light crème fraîche, to serve

preparation: 15 minutes
cooking: 20 minutes
serves: 4

nutritional values per serving
Kcals: 213 (890 kj)
Protein: 3 g
Carb: 28 g
Fat: 11 g

1 Cut the pastry into 4 pieces and roll each out thinly to a rectangle about 8 x 15 cm (3½ x 6 inches).

2 Use the point of a knife to mark a border around the pastry pieces, 1 cm (½ inch) from the edge. Lay the apple slices inside the marked square, brush with a little butter, then bake in a preheated oven, 200°C (400°F), Gas Mark 6, for 15 minutes. Remove from the oven, add the blackberries, then return to the oven and cook for a further 5 minutes.

3 Remove the tartlets from the oven and brush with a little apricot jam. Cool, then serve with a little yogurt or light crème fraîche.

nutritional tip
Eating blackberries can help boost your immune system. They are also good for combating memory loss as we get older, so tuck in now and you might never forget where you left the car keys again.

tip
If blackberries are unavailable you can use the same quantity of blueberries or raspberries.

Raspberry and passion fruit fool

200 ml (7 fl oz) light evaporated milk, chilled overnight
1 tablespoon caster sugar
450 g (14½ oz) raspberries
flesh of 2 passion fruit

preparation: 10 minutes, plus overnight chilling
serves: 4

nutritional values per serving
Kcals: 98 (414 kj)
Protein: 6 g
Carb: 14 g
Fat: 2 g

1 In a large bowl whip together the evaporated milk and sugar until the mixture is thick and fluffy.

2 Process half the raspberries in a food processor or blender until smooth, then stir into the whipped evaporated milk with the whole raspberries and the passion fruit. Chill overnight then spoon into serving dishes and serve.

Banana and chocolate microwave sponge pudding

100 g (3½ oz) butter or polyunsaturated margarine, plus extra for greasing
100 g (3½ oz) self-raising flour, plus extra for dusting
75 g (3 oz) caster sugar
2 eggs
few drops of vanilla extract
50 g (2 oz) dark chocolate drops
2 bananas, sliced

preparation: 10 minutes
cooking: 5 minutes
serves: 4

nutritional values per serving
Kcals: 494 (2069 kj)
Protein: 7 g
Carb: 58 g
Fat: 28 g

1 In a large bowl beat together the butter or margarine, flour, sugar, eggs and vanilla extract until smooth, then fold in the chocolate drops.

2 Lightly grease and flour a 600 ml (1 pint) pudding basin, layer in the banana, then pour over the sponge mixture.

3 Cover with clingfilm, then cook in the microwave on high for 4–5 minutes. Remove the clingfilm immediately and let the pudding cool in the dish for 5 minutes before turning out on to a serving plate.

Fruity bread and butter pudding

25 g (1 oz) butter
4 thick slices of Granary bread, each cut into 4 triangles
50 g (2 oz) ready-to-eat dried apricots, chopped
4 dried figs, chopped
50 g (2 oz) sultanas
3 eggs, beaten
300 ml (½ pint) milk
100 ml (3½ fl oz) single cream
pinch of nutmeg

preparation: 15 minutes, plus standing
cooking: about 30 minutes
serves: 4

nutritional values per serving
Kcals: 419 (1766 kj)
Protein: 15 g
Carb: 54 g
Fat: 18 g

1 Butter the bread slices and lightly butter an ovenproof dish or pudding basin. Place a layer of bread in the base of the dish or basin and sprinkle over some of the fruit. Repeat until all the bread and fruit is used up.

2 In a bowl whisk together the remaining ingredients and pour into the dish or basin, aiming to soak all the bread. Allow to stand for 30 minutes until all the liquid is soaked up, then bake in a preheated oven, 200°C (400°F), Gas Mark 6, for about 30 minutes until golden and risen.

tip

For a change you could use a mixture of fresh fruit to suit your taste, or use whatever you have to hand.

Simple lemon and lime cheesecake

6 oaty biscuits, roughly crushed
300 ml (½ pint) vanilla or natural yogurt
200 g (7 oz) light cream cheese
grated rind and juice of 1 lime
grated rind and juice of 1 lemon
2 tablespoons caster sugar
fresh fruit, chopped, to serve

preparation: 10 minutes
serves: 4

nutritional values per serving
Kcals: 287 (1208 kj)
Protein: 10 g
Carb: 37 g
Fat: 12 g

Divide the biscuits among 4 serving dishes. Beat together the remaining ingredients and spoon on to the biscuits. Serve immediately with some fresh fruit of your choice.

Rich chocolate mousse

150 g (5 oz) plain dark chocolate
2 large eggs, separated
4 tablespoons double cream, whipped to form soft peaks
25 g (1 oz) caster sugar
to serve
fresh fruit, chopped
light crème fraîche or cream

preparation: 15 minutes, plus chilling
cooking: 2–5 minutes
serves: 4

nutritional values per serving
Kcals: 398 (1660 kj)
Protein: 6 g
Carb: 32 g
Fat: 29 g

1 Place the chocolate in a heatproof bowl and set over a saucepan of barely simmering water until melted. Alternatively, melt the chocolate in the microwave on high for 1–2 minutes.

2 Remove the chocolate from the heat and allow to cool for a couple of minutes, then beat in the egg yolks and cream. In a clean bowl whisk the egg whites until they form soft peaks, then add the sugar and continue to whisk until stiff peaks are formed.

3 Gently fold the egg whites into the chocolate mixture, then spoon into 4 tall glasses or ramekins. Chill in the refrigerator for at least 2 hours. Serve with some fresh fruit and a spoonful of light crème fraîche or cream.

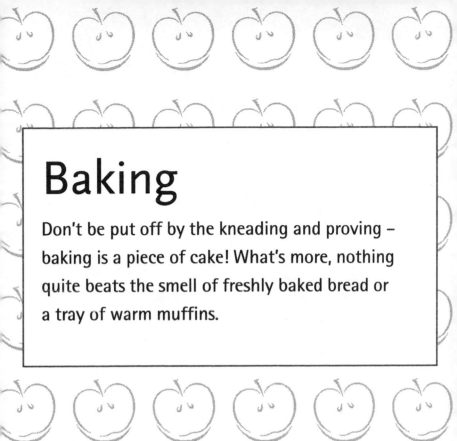

Baking

Don't be put off by the kneading and proving – baking is a piece of cake! What's more, nothing quite beats the smell of freshly baked bread or a tray of warm muffins.

Apple and apricot muffins

100 g (3½ oz) plain wholemeal flour
150 g (5 oz) plain flour
1 teaspoon baking powder
1 teaspoon bicarbonate of soda
2 tablespoons golden caster sugar
100 g (3½ oz) ready-to-eat dried apricots, chopped
½ teaspoon ground cinnamon
2 red dessert apples, peeled, cored and chopped
1 egg, beaten
50 g (2 oz) polyunsaturated margarine, melted
200 ml (7 fl oz) skimmed milk

preparation: 20 minutes
cooking: 15–20 minutes
makes: 12

nutritional values per serving
Kcals: 143 (603 kj)
Protein: 4 g
Carb: 24 g
Fat: 4 g

1 Place 12 large muffin cases in a muffin tin. Sift together the flours, baking powder and bicarbonate of soda into a large bowl, tipping any bran in the sieve into the bowl. Stir in the sugar, apricots, cinnamon and apples.

2 In a separate bowl whisk together the remaining ingredients, then gently stir into the flour mixture, making sure you don't beat too much as this will spoil the end result.

3 Spoon the mixture into the muffin cases and bake in a preheated oven, 200°C (400°F), Gas Mark 6, for 15–20 minutes. Cool a little and serve.

nutritional tip
Eating an apple with your lunch or as an afternoon snack can help stop sugar cravings. Research has also found that the fruit contains anti-carcinogenic properties: all the more reason for you to enjoy an apple a day.

Banana bread

75 g (3 oz) polyunsaturated margarine, plus extra for greasing
100 g (3½ oz) soft brown sugar
2 large eggs, beaten
3 large bananas, roughly mashed
75 g (3 oz) dates, roughly chopped
50 g (2 oz) walnuts, chopped
200 ml (7 fl oz) buttermilk
250 g (8 oz) plain wholemeal flour
1 teaspoon bicarbonate of soda

preparation: 15 minutes
cooking: 1–1¼ hours
serves: 12

nutritional values per serving
Kcals: 238 (1000 kj)
Protein 6 g
Carb: 34 g
Fat: 10 g

1 Lightly grease and line an 875 g (1¾ lb) loaf tin. In a large bowl beat together the margarine and sugar until light and fluffy. Beat in the eggs, a little at a time, then stir in the bananas, dates, walnuts and buttermilk. Fold in the flour and bicarbonate of soda.

2 Spoon the mixture into the prepared tin, then bake in a preheated oven, 180°C (350°F), Gas Mark 4, for 1-1¼ hours until a skewer comes out clean when inserted. Leave to cool, then serve.

Coconut cookies

75 g (3 oz) cornmeal (polenta)
40 g (1½ oz) plain wholemeal flour
½ teaspoon baking powder
75 g (3 oz) icing sugar
50 g (2 oz) butter, cubed and chilled
50 g (2 oz) desiccated coconut
few drops of vanilla extract
2 egg yolks
50 g (2 oz) plain dark chocolate

preparation: 15 minutes, plus chilling
cooking: 12 minutes
makes: 18

nutritional values per serving
Kcals: 97 (407 kj)
Protein: 1 g
Carb: 11 g
Fat: 6 g

1 Line 2 baking sheets with baking parchment. In a bowl stir together the cornmeal, flour, baking powder and sugar, then rub in the butter using your fingertips until the mixture resembles fine breadcrumbs. Stir through the coconut, then the vanilla extract and egg yolks to combine. Form into a firm dough, then roll into a sausage 5 cm (2 inches) in diameter. Wrap in clingfilm and chill in the refrigerator for 30 minutes.

2 Cut the dough sausage into 18 slices and place them well apart on the prepared baking sheets. Bake in a preheated oven, 180°C (350°F), Gas Mark 4, for 7–8 minutes until golden. Leave to cool on the baking sheets.

3 Break the chocolate into pieces and put them in a bowl over a saucepan of lightly simmering water until the chocolate has melted. Drizzle over the cookies using the back of a spoon.

Fruit and nut bars

100 g (3½ oz) butter or polyunsaturated margarine, plus extra for
    greasing
4 tablespoons maple syrup
2 tablespoon soft light brown sugar
150 g (5 oz) jumbo oats
100 g (3½ oz) oatmeal
50 g (2 oz) chopped mixed nuts
150 g (5 oz) mixed dried fruit (such as figs, dates, apricots and
    cranberries), chopped
2 tablespoons sunflower seeds

preparation: 10 minutes
cooking: 15 minutes
makes: 8

nutritional values per serving
Kcals: 368 (1542 kj)
Protein: 6 g
Carb: 46 g
Fat: 19 g

1 Lightly grease and base-line a 20 cm (8 inch) square, nonstick baking tin. In a saucepan melt together the butter, syrup and sugar. Stir in all the remaining ingredients, except the sunflower seeds, then press the mixture into the prepared tin.

2 Sprinkle over the sunflower seeds, then bake in a preheated oven, 200°C (400°F), Gas Mark 6, for 15 minutes until golden. Mark into 8 bars. Cool, then serve.

nutritional tip

Sunflower seeds are rich in omega-3 and omega-6 fatty acids, which can help protect against heart disease. They also contain the unsaturated fats that lower blood cholesterol, so they're a bit of a super seed! Try sprinkling them over salads or cereal.

Mixed seed rolls

450 g (14½ oz) Granary flour, plus extra for dusting
pinch of salt
7 g (¼ oz) sachet easy-blend dried yeast
100 g (3½ oz) mixed seeds (such as sesame, sunflower and
    pumpkin)
2 tablespoons clear honey
250 ml (8 fl oz) hand-hot water
oil, for oiling

preparation: 20 minutes, plus proving
cooking: 20 minutes
makes: 8

nutritional values per serving
Kcals: 270 (1140 kj)
Protein: 10 g
Carb: 44 g
Fat: 7 g

1 In a large bowl mix together the flour, salt, yeast and the mixed seeds (reserve 1 tablespoon). Stir half the honey into the water, then pour into the flour and form into a soft dough.

2 Tip out the dough on to a lightly floured surface and knead for 5 minutes. Place in a lightly oiled bowl, cover with a damp cloth and leave to prove in a warm place until doubled in size.

3 Re-knead the dough for 5 minutes, then divide into 8 pieces. Knead to form rolls, then place on a baking sheet, cover and leave to prove again until doubled in size.

4 Brush over the remaining honey and sprinkle over the reserved seeds. Bake the rolls in a preheated oven, 200°C (400°F), Gas Mark 6, for 20 minutes until they are golden and sound hollow when tapped.

Rye bread

450 g (14½ oz) strong white flour, plus extra for dusting
450 g (14½ oz) rye flour
2 x 7 g (¼ oz) sachets easy-blend dried yeast
2 teaspoons caraway seeds
1 teaspoon salt
4 tablespoons oil, plus extra for oiling
1 tablespoon clear honey
4 tablespoons low-fat natural yogurt
550 ml (17½ fl oz) tepid water

preparation: 20 minutes, plus proving
cooking: 30–35 minutes
makes: 2 x 500 g (1 lb) loaves

nutritional values per serving
Kcals: 152 (646 kj)
Protein: 4 g
Carb: 30 g
Fat: 3 g

1 In a large bowl mix together the flours, yeast, caraway seeds and salt. Stir the remaining ingredients into the water, then gradually stir into the flour mixture to form a soft dough.

2 Tip out the dough on to a lightly floured surface and knead for 5 minutes until smooth. Place the dough in a lightly oiled bowl, cover with a damp cloth and leave to prove in a warm place for 1 hour until it has doubled in size.

3 Re-knead the dough, divide into 2 equal pieces and shape each into an oval loaf. Place the loaves on lightly floured baking sheets, cover with a damp cloth and leave to prove again until the loaves have doubled in size.

4 Slash the tops of the loaves a few times with a sharp knife, then bake in a preheated oven, 200°C (400°F), Gas Mark 6, for 30–35 minutes until golden and sounding hollow when tapped. Leave to cool on a wire rack, then serve.

Rustic nutty seed loaf

450 g (14½ oz) wholemeal flour, plus extra for dusting
1 teaspoon salt
100 g (3½ oz) mixed seeds (such as pumpkin, sunflower and poppy)
25 g (1 oz) bulgar wheat
1½ x 7 g (¼ oz) sachets easy-blend dried yeast
50 g (2 oz) mixed nuts (such as hazelnuts and walnuts), chopped
6 spring onions, sliced
50 g (2 oz) Parmesan cheese, freshly grated
1 tablespoon clear honey
300 ml (½ pint) warm water
oil, for oiling

preparation: 15 minutes, plus proving
cooking: 30–35 minutes
makes: 1 large loaf

nutritional values per serving
Kcals: 165 (697 kj)
Protein: 8 g
Carb: 23 g
Fat: 7 g

1 In a large bowl mix together all the ingredients, except the honey and water. Blend the honey with the water, then stir into the flour, mix and form into a dough.

2 Tip out the dough on to a lightly floured surface and knead for 5 minutes until smooth. Place the dough in a lightly oiled bowl, cover with a damp cloth and leave to prove in a warm place for 2 hours until it has doubled in size.

3 Re-knead the dough, shape into a round and place on a baking sheet. Cover with a damp cloth and leave to prove again for 1 hour. Bake the loaf in a preheated oven, 220°C (425°F), Gas Mark 7, for 30–35 minutes until it sounds hollow when tapped.

Orange and sultana scones

125 g (4 oz) self-raising flour, plus extra for dusting
100 g (3½ oz) wholemeal self-raising flour
2 teaspoons baking powder
50 g (2 oz) butter, cubed and chilled
50 g (2 oz) sultanas
1 tablespoon caster sugar
grated rind of 1 orange
1 egg
about 125 ml (4 fl oz) milk, plus extra for brushing
to serve
cream cheese
fresh strawberries (optional)

preparation: 20 minutes
cooking: about 10 minutes
makes: 12

nutritional values per serving
Kcals: 120 (505 kj)
Protein: 3 g
Carb: 18 g
Fat: 4 g

1 Sift the flours and baking powder into a large bowl, tipping any bran in the sieve into the bowl. Rub in the butter using your fingertips until the mixture resembles fine breadcrumbs, then stir in the sultanas, sugar and orange rind.

2 Break the egg into a measuring jug and beat with a fork. Make up to 150 ml (¼ pint) with milk, then pour into the flour mixture and bring together to form a soft dough, adding a little extra milk if the dough is too dry.

3 Gently press the dough into a 1 cm (½ inch) thick round. Stamp out about 12 scones, place on lightly floured baking sheets and brush with a little milk. Bake in a preheated oven, 220°C (425°F), Gas Mark 7, for about 10 minutes until risen and golden.

4 Cool the scones on a wire rack, then serve that day to enjoy them at their best. Serve with a little cream cheese and fresh strawberries, if liked, to bring down the overall GI.

Sesame seed oatcakes

200 g (7 oz) oatmeal
1 tablespoon sesame seeds
pinch of salt
pinch of bicarbonate of soda
1 tablespoon olive oil
2–3 tablespoons hot water
flour, for dusting

preparation: 10 minutes
cooking: about 10 minutes
makes: about 12

nutritional values per serving
Kcals: 79 (330 kj)
Protein: 2 g
Carb: 11 g
Fat: 3 g

1 In a bowl mix together all the ingredients to form a firm dough, adding a little extra water if necessary. The mixture will be very crumbly, so just keep pressing it back together.

2 Roll out the mixture on a lightly floured surface as thinly as you can. Cut out triangles or 7 cm (3 inch) rounds and place on baking sheets. Bake in a preheated oven, 180°C (350°F), Gas Mark 4, for about 10 minutes until golden and firm. Cool on a wire rack.

Pesto and sesame seed pastry twists

250 g (8 oz) shortcrust pastry
flour, for dusting
2 tablespoons pesto
2 tablespoons milk or a little beaten egg
2 tablespoons sesame seeds

preparation: 10 minutes
cooking: 8–10 minutes
makes: 15

nutritional values per serving
Kcals: 94 (390 kj)
Protein: 2 g
Carb: 8 g
Fat: 6 g

1 Roll out the pastry on a lightly floured surface to a 25 cm (10 inch) square. Spoon over the pesto and spread out to the edges. Cut the pastry into 15 strips.

2 Twist the strips and place them on a baking sheet. Brush with a little milk or egg and sprinkle over the sesame seeds. Bake in a preheated oven, 200°C (400°F), Gas Mark 6, for 8–10 minutes until golden. Leave to cool on a wire rack.

Parmesan and Caerphilly biscuits

125 g (4 oz) plain wholemeal flour

75 g (3 oz) butter, cubed and chilled, or polyunsaturated margarine, cut into pieces

2 tablespoons cornmeal (polenta)

100 g (3½ oz) Caerphilly cheese, or other crumbly cheese, crumbled

50 g (2 oz) Parmesan cheese, freshly grated

50 g (2 oz) ready-to-eat dried apricots, chopped

1 egg yolk

cheese or fresh fruit (such as apples or pears), to serve

preparation: 10 minutes, plus chilling
cooking: 10–12 minutes
makes: 20

nutritional values per serving
Kcals: 90 (373 kj)
Protein: 3 g
Carb: 6 g
Fat: 6 g

1 Sift the flour into a bowl and rub in the butter or margarine with your fingertips until the mixture resembles fine breadcrumbs. Stir in the cornmeal, cheeses and apricots, then add the egg yolk and bring the mixture together to form a ball. It will be very crumbly, so just keep pressing it back together.

2 Roll the ball into a sausage about 5 cm (2 inches) in diameter, wrap in clingfilm, then chill in the refrigerator for 30 minutes. Cut the dough sausage into 20 slices, place on baking sheets and bake in a preheated oven, 200°C (400°F), Gas Mark 6, for 10–12 minutes until golden. Cool, then serve with cheese or fresh fruit to keep down the GI.

index

Acknowledgements

Executive Editor **Nicola Hill**
Editor **Charlotte Macey**
Executive Art Editor **Joanna MacGregor**
Page make-up **Dorchester Typesetting Group Ltd**
Production Manager **Ian Paton**